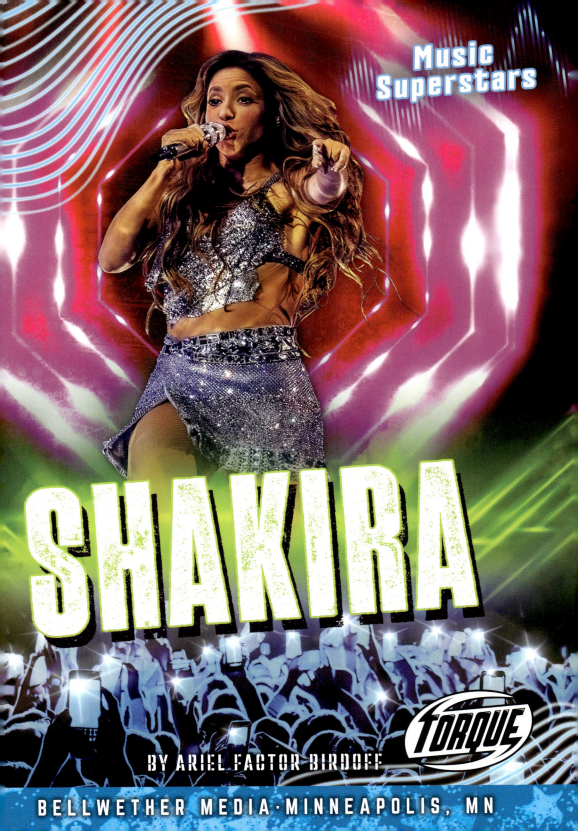

Torque brims with excitement perfect for thrill-seekers of all kinds. Discover daring survival skills, explore uncharted worlds, and marvel at mighty engines and extreme sports. In *Torque* books, anything can happen. Are you ready?

This edition first published in 2026 by Bellwether Media, Inc.

No part of this publication may be reproduced in whole or in part without written permission of the publisher. For information regarding permission, write to Bellwether Media, Inc., Attention: Permissions Department, 3500 American Blvd W, Suite 150, Bloomington, MN 55431.

Library of Congress Cataloging-in-Publication Data

Names: Birdoff, Ariel Factor, author.
Title: Shakira / by Ariel Factor Birdoff.
Description: Minneapolis, MN : Bellwether Media, 2026. | Series: Music superstars | Includes bibliographical references and index. | Audience: Ages 7-12 | Audience: Grades 4-6 | Summary: "Engaging images accompany information about Shakira. The combination of high-interest subject matter and light text is intended for students in grades 3 through 7"-Provided by publisher"– Provided by publisher.
Identifiers: LCCN 2025001554 (print) | LCCN 2025001555 (ebook) | ISBN 9798893045031 (library binding) | ISBN 9798893046410 (ebook)
Subjects: LCSH: Shakira–Juvenile literature. | Singers–Latin America–Biography–Juvenile literature. | LCGFT: Biographies.
Classification: LCC ML3930.S46 B57 2026 (print) | LCC ML3930.S46 (ebook) | DDC 782.42164092 [B]–dc23/eng/20250115
LC record available at https://lccn.loc.gov/2025001554
LC ebook record available at https://lccn.loc.gov/2025001555

Text copyright © 2026 by Bellwether Media, Inc. TORQUE and associated logos are trademarks and/or registered trademarks of Bellwether Media, Inc. Bellwether Media is a division of FlutterBee Education Group.

Editor: Rachael Barnes   Designer: Josh Brink

Printed in the United States of America, North Mankato, MN.

TABLE OF CONTENTS

The Queen of Latin Music	4
Who Is Shakira?	6
An Early Start	8
Whenever, Wherever	12
Global Superstar	20
Glossary	22
To Learn More	23
Index	24

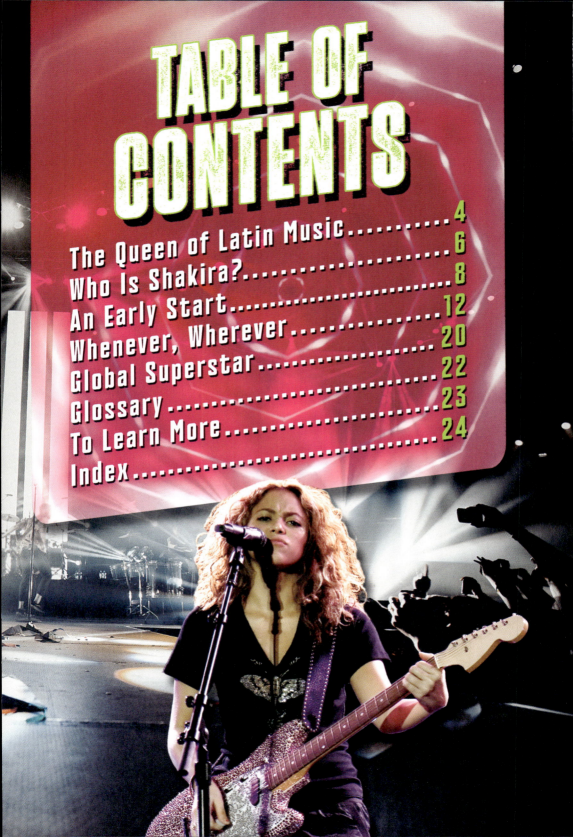

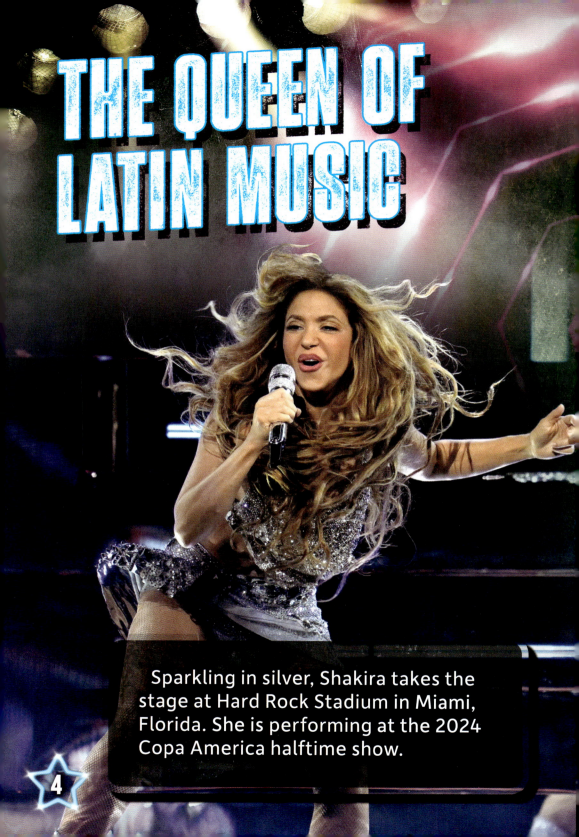

THE QUEEN OF LATIN MUSIC

Sparkling in silver, Shakira takes the stage at Hard Rock Stadium in Miami, Florida. She is performing at the 2024 Copa America halftime show.

Lights flash and fans cheer as Shakira dances and **belts** "Hips Don't Lie." She and her backup dancers perform three more of her hit songs. Shakira shines!

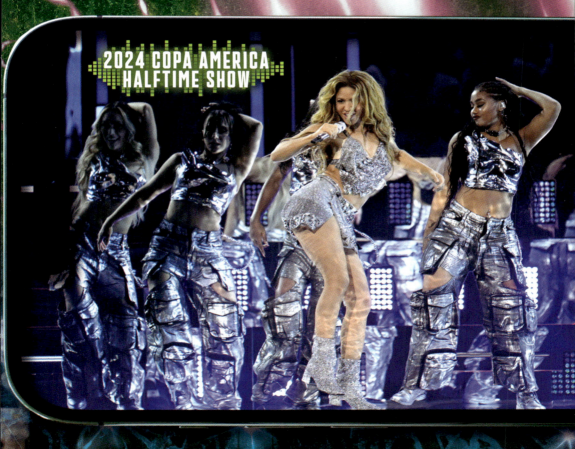

2024 COPA AMERICA HALFTIME SHOW

WHO IS SHAKIRA?

Shakira is a Colombian singer-songwriter and dancer. She sings in both English and Spanish. Shakira's career has lasted more than 30 years. She is one of the most popular Latin American artists in the world!

SHAKIRA

Birthday
February 2, 1977

Hometown
Barranquilla, Colombia

Types of Music
Latin, pop, rock

First Hit in English
"Whenever, Wherever"

She is also a **philanthropist**. Much of her work focuses on education and support for children in need.

AN EARLY START

Shakira Isabel Mebarak Ripoll was born in Barranquilla, Colombia. Her father is Lebanese and her mother is Colombian. Shakira began singing and belly-dancing when she was very young.

A YOUNG POET

Shakira wrote her first poem at age 4! It is called *La Rosa De Cristal*. In English, the title means "The Crystal Rose."

At 10 years old, she began writing her own music and entering contests. Shakira knew then that she wanted to be a performer.

When she was 13 years old, Shakira signed a **contract** with Sony Music Colombia. Her first two albums, *Magia* and *Peligro*, did not do well.

SHAKIRA PERFUME!

Shakira started her own perfume line in 2010. It is called Shakira Perfumes!

FAVORITES

Color
lilac

Food dish
mojarra frita

Actor
Hugh Grant

Book
The Prophet by Khalil Gibran

Her third album, *Pies Descalzos*, was released in 1995. It featured a mix of Latin, rock, and Arabic music. It went on to sell more than 5 million copies!

11

WHENEVER, WHEREVER

SHAKIRA WITH HER PARENTS

When Shakira was 20 years old, her family moved to the United States. She taught herself to write and sing songs in English.

Shakira **released** her fourth album in 1998. *Dónde Están Los Ladrones?* hit number one on the **Billboard** Top Latin Albums chart!

In 1999, Shakira performed on the *MTV Unplugged* TV show. The live album from the show won a **Grammy Award**! In 2001, Shakira released her first English-language album. *Laundry Service* **debuted** at number three on the *Billboard* 200 chart!

2001 GRAMMY AWARDS

AWARDS

as of February 2025

6 MTV Video Music Awards

4 Grammy Awards

14 Latin Grammy Awards

8 *Billboard* Music Awards

Shakira released her next two albums in 2005. *Fijación Oral, Vol. 1* won Shakira her second Grammy.

Shakira went on tour and released another live album. In 2009, she released her eighth album, *She Wolf*.

TRY EVERYTHING!

Shakira was the voice of Gazelle in *Zootopia* in 2016. She sang "Try Everything."

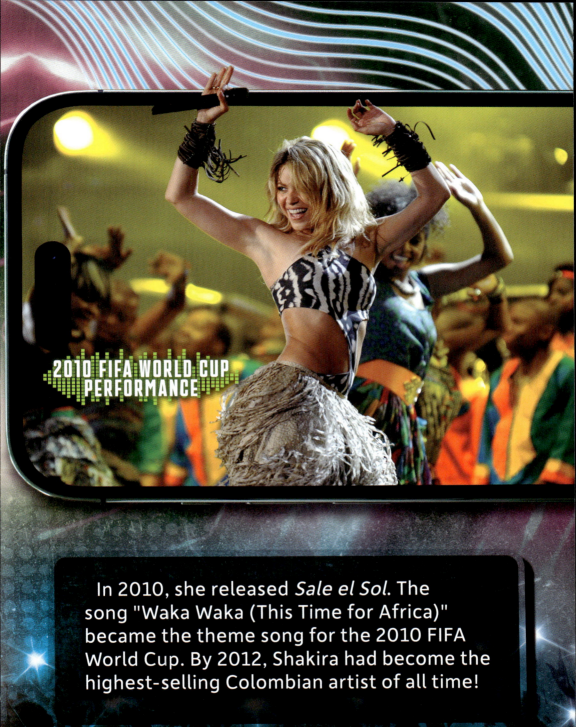

2010 FIFA WORLD CUP PERFORMANCE

In 2010, she released *Sale el Sol*. The song "Waka Waka (This Time for Africa)" became the theme song for the 2010 FIFA World Cup. By 2012, Shakira had become the highest-selling Colombian artist of all time!

Shakira continued making albums and going on tour. In 2020, she performed with Jennifer Lopez at the Super Bowl halftime show! In 2023, Shakira was named the *Billboard* Latin Woman of the Year.

Shakira's 12th album was released in 2024. *Las Mujeres Ya No Lloran* was **streamed** globally more than 10 million times in one day. It went on to win a Grammy!

TIMELINE

– 1991 –
Shakira releases her first album, *Magia*

– 2001 –
Shakira releases her first English-language album, *Laundry Service*

SHAKIRA PERFORMING WITH JENNIFER LOPEZ

– 2010 –
Shakira performs "Waka Waka (This Time for Africa)" at the FIFA World Cup

– 2020 –
Shakira performs with Jennifer Lopez at the Super Bowl halftime show

– 2025 –
Shakira wins a Grammy for her album *Las Mujeres Ya No Lloran*

GLOBAL SUPERSTAR

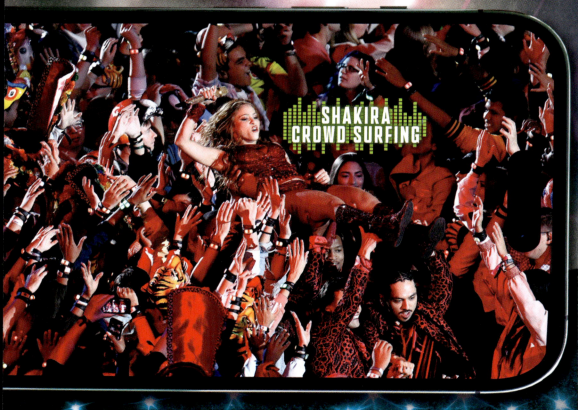

SHAKIRA CROWD SURFING

Shakira has fans all over the world. She is loved for her powerful music, amazing dance moves, and incredible kindness.

PLAYLIST

"Whenever, Wherever"
(2001)

"Hips Don't Lie"
(2005)

"Beautiful Liar"
(2007)

"Waka Waka
(This Time for Africa)"
(2010)

"Try Everything"
(2016)

"Cohete"
(2024)

When she was a child, Shakira promised to use her future fame to help children. She has kept her promise! Shakira works with **UNICEF**. She also started a **foundation**. Her talent and kindness have made her a superstar!

21

GLOSSARY

belts—sings in a forceful way

Billboard—related to a well-known music news magazine and website that ranks songs and albums

contract—an agreement between two or more people

debuted—was introduced or released for the first time

foundation—an organization that helps people and communities

Grammy Award—an award given by the Recording Academy of the United States for an achievement in music; Grammy Awards are also called Grammys.

philanthropist—a person who gives money and time to help make life better for other people

released—made music available for listening

streamed—listened to or played online

UNICEF—a part of the United Nations that helps children in need; the United Nations is a group of nations that work together for world peace and safety.

TO LEARN MORE

AT THE LIBRARY

Birdoff, Ariel Factor. *Bad Bunny*. New York, N.Y.: Bellwether Media, 2025.

Reynoso-Morris, Alyssa. *Bold, Brilliant, and Latine*. London, U.K.: Wide Eyed Editions, 2025.

Sánchez Vegara, Maria Isabel. *Shakira*. London, U.K.: Frances Lincoln Children's Books, 2023.

ON THE WEB

FACTSURFER

Factsurfer.com gives you a safe, fun way to find more information.

1. Go to www.factsurfer.com.

2. Enter "Shakira" into the search box and click 🔍.

3. Select your book cover to see a list of related content.

INDEX

albums, 10, 11, 13, 14, 15, 16, 17, 18
awards, 14, 15, 18
Billboard, 13, 14, 18
childhood, 8, 9, 10, 21
Colombia, 6, 8, 17
contract, 10
Copa America, 4–5
dancer, 5, 6, 8, 20
family, 8, 12
fans, 5, 20
favorites, 11
FIFA World Cup, 17
foundation, 21
languages, 6, 12, 14
Lopez, Jennifer, 18, 19
MTV Unplugged, 14

perfume line, 10
philanthropist, 7
playlist, 21
poem, 9
profile, 7
sales, 11, 17
songs, 5, 12, 16, 17
Sony Music Colombia, 10
streams, 18
Super Bowl, 18
timeline, 18–19
tours, 16, 18
types of music, 11
UNICEF, 21
United States, 12
Zootopia, 16

The images in this book are reproduced through the courtesy of: Chris Arjoon/ Alamy, front cover; Catsense, front cover (light effect); Taya Ovod, pp. 2-3; Dario Sabljak, p. 3; JUAN MABROMATA/ AFP/ Getty Images, pp. 4, 5; Joaquin Corchero/ Europa Press/ Getty Images, p. 6; Susan Walsh/ AP Images, p. 7; William Volcov/ ZUMA Press Wire/ Alamy, p. 7 (VIP pass); M. Caulfield/ WireImage/ Getty Images, p. 8; BERTRAND PARRES/ AFP/ Getty Images, p. 9; Europa Press Entertainment/ Getty Images, p. 10; KMazur/ WireImage/ Getty Images, p. 11; Elena11, p. 11 (paint swatch); Luis Echeverri Urrea, p. 11 (*mojarra frita*); Featureflash Photo Agency, p. 11 (Hugh Grant); w:en:EamonnPKeane, p. 11 (*The Prophet*); ROBERTO SCHMIDT/ AFP/ Getty Images, pp. 12, 13; Vince Bucci/ AFP/ Getty Images, p. 14; TIMOTHY A. CLARY/ AFP/ Getty Images, p. 15; WFDJ_Stock, p. 15 (MTV Video Music Award); CarlosVdeHabsburgo/ Wikipedia, p. 15 (Grammy Awards); Kathy Hutchins, p. 15 (*Billboard* Music Award); Stephane Cardinale/ Corbis/ Getty Images, p. 16; Stuart Franklin/ Getty Images, p. 17; Paul Kitagaki Jr./ ZUMA Wire/ Alamy, p. 19; BWM, pp. 18, 19, 21; ANGELA WEISS/ AFP/ Getty Images, p. 20; VALERIE MACON / AFP/ Getty Images, pp. 20-21; Niccolo Guasti/ Getty Images, p. 23.